Nakedly Covered:
a collection of haiku

by
Randy C. Rogers
a.k.a.
"freedom clay"

"Love takes off the mask we fear we cannot live without and know we cannot live within."

James Baldwin

foreword

It was 2004-2005 on the campus of North Carolina Central University when I met this intelligent and aesthetically pleasing gentleman by the name of Randy Rogers. I was a volunteer for his Men's Health Initiative, and he taught me so much about implementing health programs on college campuses. When the program ended, I then went on to be a Research Assistant at the UNC Lineberger Comprehensive Cancer Center and to my surprise, I walked into the building and was so elated when I saw a familiar face. He and I worked on two of the projects together, but I looked at him as more of a mentor rather than a colleague. I was still a student and I was trying to get my feet wet in the field of public health, so I soaked in as much information from all the professionals in the room. However, Randy never treated me as such. That was the type of person Randy Rogers has and has always been treating co-workers as equals and not as subordinates. Hence, when I graduated and worked alongside him at the Durham

County Department of Public Health, it was more of a familial feel which is why I now refer to him as my Brother.

My Brother has always found art in any and everything. I still remember when he started painting, he would paint these beautiful sunflowers that looked as if they each had their own personalities. When he branched out and started curating series paintings, I said to him, "Brother you are very talented, and you can do big things with this." I believe in supporting those who support you and that is how our friendship has always been. Our relationship is something special: no one can come between us. When he developed the *"Love Series,"* I went to him with an idea of what I would like for him to paint and in true Randy fashion, he did it for me. I was able to afford a couple of his originals in the beginning but now that he is an international artist, I have to swing on a pole just to be able to afford even the littlest painting. However, I do purchase other pieces since he has expanded his brand into merchandising. Along with his artistry with paint, he has a gift with words. When giving advice or even just having casual conversation, he would put things in a different perspective that would make you think. I believe it was back in 2016 when Brother started *"freedom clay talk,"* where he would post on social media just random things about life, love, personal growth and relationships. His posts were more sporadic at the time but then immediately became more frequent. I remember us being out at dinner or for drinks and we were talking about his next projects and I joked with him, *"Brother when are you going to come out with your damn book, I'm ready for it now, shit?!"* As we laughed together, he said to me, *"Sis, everyone keeps asking me that and I promise you it is coming."* I believe it was about a year later, he came out with his first literary baby, *"Inspirational and Provocative Moments on Faith, Self-Love & Relationships."* This book was an accumulation of his posts formulated into a multifunctional piece of work. In 2018, he approached me asking if I could serve as Co-Editor on his second book. Just when we were about to get started, we both were struck by a surprising death in our families. I don't know how my Brother fought through his grief and still was able to push through and finish it in about two months. His strength is incomparable and inspiring at the same time. *"575: a collection of haiku by freedom clay"* was such a great project to work on and experiencing that with my Brother was just simply amazing. I was elated to have been a part of bringing his vision to life.

Words cannot express how proud I am of my Brother. He has done so many amazing things over the years and just continues to be such an influence. I adore him for he is, I love him for who he will continue to be, genuine and authentically…freedom clay.

Peace and Blessings,

Lil Sis….April McCoy

testimonial

"I've known rivers: I've known rivers ancient as the world and older than the flow of human blood in human veins. My soul has grown deep like the rivers."

Langston Hughes

Taking into account his excellent wordplay, freedom clay not only celebrates the joys of authentic blackness, but bares the intricacies of his deep soul with touching poignancy. Stylistically unapologetic, and fantastically in touch with his roots, he manages to provoke the gamut of emotions effortlessly.

D'Moreo Balthazar

acknowledgements

Hallelujah is unequivocally the HIGHEST praise and I'm eternally humbled and grateful to be a perpetual recipient of The Most High's unmerited favor, grace and mercy. Simply, I owe YOU me.

Sister Sister aka my dearest April, mere words simply aren't sufficient enough to describe what you mean to me. Beyond the effortless and sacred bond we share as friends, chosen siblings and colleagues, you are a woman of exceptional beauty, character, intelligence, loyalty, integrity and strength. This is the second project where you have served as my co-editor and the chief formatting and layout engineer. There are few people that I would trust to translate my creative visions: you are one of them. Thank you for being remarkably and uniquely YOU. Most importantly, thank you for being one of my most cherished confidants. You are one of the reasons this beloved project was realized. Now, let's CELEBRATE!!! Here's to LOVE...here's to LIFE...here's to US!!!

dedication

This compilation of love in haiku is dedicated to those continuing to manage grief and loss experienced and to Black men and boys who have questioned your purpose and the value of your existence. You are seen and loved beyond measure, despite what the world constantly shows and tell us about ourselves. We matter.

"Sir James Baldwin"
One of my heroes
Celebrated after death
For being himself.

introduction

Uncertainty, vulnerability, pandemic, infectious, oppression, discrimination, mortality, grief, healing, inequity, equality, discrimination, co-morbidity, alone, together, face masks, social distancing, faith and hope are some of the words that are being used as we continue to make meaning of the global and domestic impact of COVID-19 and racism: two egregious public health issues. As we continue to learn effective ways to contain and resolve these dis-eases, we are also finding creative ways to co-exist and support each other during these tumultuous times. Imagine that?!?! Although we are expected to be fully clothed and masked to protect ourselves, we are also experiencing a level of emotional nakedness and vulnerability. Introducing my latest collection of haiku...

"Nakedly Covered"

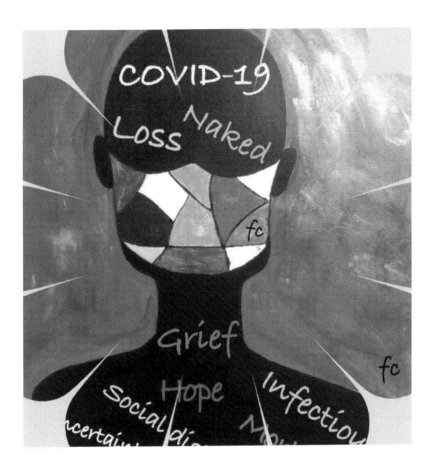

"Nakedly Covered"

is a collection of love via structured words paying homage to Black men and boys, along with a myriad of thoughts about love, living, legacy, wonder, healing and humanity in haiku.

table of contents

"575 Memories"

Create memories
That will bring you a lifetime
Of joy, peace and love.

"Bull City Luv"

Medicine city
Re-imagining itself
With creative minds.

freedom clay

"Bull City Facelift"

Durham is changing
In multiple directions
While much stays the same.

"Rogers Family & Friends"

Family of choice
Family of origin
Family matters.

"Dining with Fam"

Break bread with loved ones
Full of laughter and good food
It's intimacy.

"Blood Brothers"

He is my brother
The sons of Constance Rogers
We're her legacy.

"My Brother's Keeper"

You can lean on me
I am my brother's keeper
Together, we stand.

"M. Scottica"

Devoted Brotha
They call him daddy daycare
Chapter 48.

"Hazel Eyes: my Goddaughter"

She makes my heart sing
With her piercing hazel eyes
A blessing from God.

"The Real McCoy"

Sipping and jiving
On "The Real McCoy" cocktail
Honoring my sis!

"Artsy People of Color"

Diverse creatives
Showcasing their artistry
In vivid colors.

"Collaboration"

It's intentional
A process of time-effort
Working together.

"HBCU Pride"

Black pride amplified
Making lifelong connections
Familial vibes.

"Aggies Who Brunch"

Mimosas flowing
With a delectable spread
Full of blue & gold.

"Aggie Pride"

The Greensboro Four
Sat down so many could stand
Aggie TALL with pride.

"Submerging Gratitude"

As I close my eyes
And prepare to hold my breath
I'm grateful for life.

"The Little Things"

Finding the sunshine
In prepping to cook pintos
Was gratifying.

"Grateful"

I am so grateful
The universe met my needs
I was just faithful.

"Grateful Heart"

Woke up with a praise
Deep down in my heart and soul
And it feels so good.

"Grateful Reflections"

I am reflecting
And it is feeling so good
You are on my mind.

freedom clay

"Grateful, I am"

I am so grateful
This is my testimony
For God's covering.

"STILL"

My love continues
Because you're always with me
I am grateful...STILL.

"Stillness"

Choosing to be STILL
Learning to sit in silence
Can be cathartic.

"Conversations Matter"

Let's talk about it
Love yourself; protect yourself
We are ALL we got.

"Worthy"

You are not crazy
You deserve to be valued
Your BE-ing is REAL.

"I am"

I am courageous
I am bold, loved, strong and free
I am positive.

"Fruitful Mind"
Whatever we feed
And fertilize our minds with
Will most likely grow.

fc

"Laughter"

It's good for the soul
While releasing endorphins
And better when shared.

"Personal Hydration"

Pour into yourself
Until your cup overflows
Then, it's time to share.

"Self-Preservation"

It is not selfish
To protect your energy
It's an act of love.

"Potty Words"

Seen in a restroom
Conspicuously centered
Love yourself harder.

"Love Yourself"

Love on YOU today
Take a moment to feel love
There's value in it.

"My Name IS..."

Remember your name
Even when others forget
Now, speak it with love.

"Self-Care"

Take care of yourself
You cannot be reproduced
It's a humbling truth.

"The Spine"

The skeletal core
Equipped to hold our content
Take care of your spine.

"Capturing Love & Care"

Make time for self-care
And have the moments captured
Through the lens of love.

freedom clay

"I got YOU"

Having your own back
Is a self-preserving act;
Not a selfish one.

"be YOU"

You are deserving
Don't be afraid to exist
And BE your best self.

"Shine Brightly"

Lovers gonna love
And haters are gonna hate
So let your light shine.

"LOVE-JOY"

You are your best thing
Wrap yourself in love and joy
Deserving, YOU are.

"JOYful Moments"

EnJOY this lifetime
And make meaning of moments
That matter to YOU.

"Personalized Journey"

Respect your process
Do not be rushed by others
This is your journey.

"Freely Experience Joy"

Don't deny yourself
Of people, places and things
That enhance your joy.

"Cerebral Ammunition"

Your brain is a gun
Loaded possibilities
Proceed with caution.

"Mental Hygiene"

Take care of your mind
Like we tend to our bodies
Maintenance is key.

"Zen-ful Moments"

Today, be mindful
What you feed your psyche
Rest your body and mind.

"Energy Matters"

Wisely, choose battles
Because energy matters
Expend cautiously.

"Your Mind Matters"

What is on your mind
Listening without judgement
It matters to me.

"Recharge"

Take time to recharge
It's essential to wellness
Prioritize it.

"Prepare"

Preparing matters
If you don't prepare to win
Be prepared to fail.

50|

freedom clay

"Goal"

You say you want it
Do you really believe it
Then go after it.

"Try"

Go ahead; try it
Don't let FEAR paralyze you
Because you're worth it.

"Wondering or Whateva"

What if this was meant
I want to go all the way
Unafraid to soar.

"Leap of Faith"

Invest in yourself
Proceed with taking the leap
Destiny awaits.

"Keep Your Head Up"

Today, keep your head up
And know that your life has value
Because YOU matter.

"Stay Up"

A balancing act
One of the tenets of life
To survive and thrive.

"Wine Down Wednesday"

It's wine down Wednesday
And it's the perfect evening
to enjoy a glass.

"Salud"

Here's to love and life
Great health and new beginnings
Full of gratitude.

"Mental Getaway"

Choosing to escape
Suspending reality
Can be good for you.

"Don't Worry"

Do not worry now
About things you can't control
By faith, it is done.

"Strangely Untitled"

The shame of it ALL
Can conjure joyful moments
If we just let go.

"Breathing Easily"

Sitting with my thoughts
Underneath a moonlit sky
And breathing freely.

"Let it Out"

When the rage is real
And screaming is not enough
Feel it, let it out!

"Release"

Today was the day
I released and crossed the bridge
To embrace what's next.

"Prayers for Corporate Healing"

Alone together
People are suffering, still
Praying for healing.

"Hurricane Flo"

You came thru prancing
With dashing and twirling winds
Causing trees to fall.

"Face Mask"

Another layer
Protecting self & others
From COVID-19.

"Personal Protective Equipment"

Since they're essential
Universal precautions
Make it personal.

"Social Distancing"

Keeping our distance
Together, we can make it
One day at a time.

"Protection Is Personal"

Love and protect YOU
And the loved ones you carry
Now, wear your face mask.

"Smiling with my Eyez"

They can't see my smile
Smizing is the new normal
I greet with a nod.

"Signs of the Time"

It will get better
When we turn inward then out
Working together.

freedom clay

"And So It Is..."

Lawd, we will get by
I'm thanking you in advance
For what is to come.

"Contemplation"

Thinking and being
As I sit in the moment
It's already alright.

"It's Alright"

We gotta believe
Even when you can't see it
ALL will be alright.

"Quarantine Thoughts"

Feeling imprisoned
Reimagine protection
Relax, relate, release.

"Waiting & Anticipating"

You're not ready now
When you are, ALL will align
Be kind to yourself.

"Reflecting & Retreating"

Take time to step back
From the world's dissonance
Re-join when ready.

"Opposing Thoughts"

The brain is filled with
Copious information
Not always aligned.

"Your Bluez Ain't Like Mine"

The weight we carry
Is much heavier than most
Yet, we keep lifting.

"Misunderstood"

My self confidence
Is often misunderstood
Because I am Black.

"Situational Communication"

Coded languages
Are spoken regularly
When appropriate.

"Human-beings"

Yes, we're different
Yet alike in many ways
Take the time to see.

"Shades of Humanity"

All colors matter
In the rainbow hues of life
Value the promise.

freedom clay

"Strange Fruit"

Still viewed as strange fruit
Though composition varies
Black bodies matter.

"Black Bodies Matter"

Value Black bodies
The sustainers of humans
Stop policing US.

"When Black Men Smile"

When they see US smile
Bewilderment is present
They don't understand.

"We Are VISIBLE BE-INGS"

Our Black flesh matters
Objectification kills
Black men are hue-man.

"Damn YOU, Karens"

News flash white women
Check your white supremacy
Black men are human.

"Respect Black Boys"

Do you SEE Black boys?
Because they really matter
No reason needed.

freedom clay

"Black Boys Bleed Too"

They have hearts that beat
Residing in their bodies
Black boys have feelings.

"They're Watching Us"

We must protect them
Let Black boys grow up & thrive
Their lives matter too.

"Us"

Reflections of "us"
Are among those who oppress
So pay attention.

"Justice 4 Bre"

Breonna Taylor
A promising Black woman
Was senselessly killed.

"Justice for Ahmaud Arbery"

I remain speechless
Not because I am voiceless
Enough is enough.

"Truth is"

It could have been me
Most conscious Black men relate
To this succinct truth.

"1968 vs. 2020 Protests"

A change is coming
Intergenerational
Contributions made.

"Time-Warping"

Sitting here thinking
Is it the sixties again
Or twenty twenty.

"Marching 4 Justice"

National Protests
Impact public policy
Effective, they are.

"Artivism"

Visibility
Creating change thru the arts
Connecting colors.

freedom clay

"Black Man Hollering"

I want to holler!!!
It's systemic racism
Granting heinous acts.

"Mentally Strapped Black Boys"

Must they fight daily
With their guards constantly up
Just to breathe freely?

"Good Trouble"

A courageous act
Civil Disobedience
Seeks human justice.

"Just Mercy"

Hope and faith matter
In systems of injustice
This is my belief.

freedom clay

"Lock-Free"

Unlock the cell door
Oppression isn't okay
For any human.

"An Unshackled Mind"

As I lay in jail
Surrounded by concrete walls
I'm caged; yet, still FREE!

"Imprisoned Mindset"

Self-imposed shackles
Are not always visible
Though, the weight is felt.

"Civil Unrest"

Until we're treated
As "valued" human beings
Mutiny prevails.

freedom clay

"Free Black Boy Joy"

His smile was intact
As he moved courageously
Pass "law" enforcement.

"Freedom Run"

Sprinting boundlessly
Thru sugar cane enriched fields
Parole completed!

"Freedom Release"

With my arms outstretched
Black folks just want 2 b free
Of oppressive hands.

"The Cries of Black Folks"

Finally, our cries
Are shape shifting our nation
They are being heard.

"Black Men Can"

Temporarily
Sheltered by the woes of life
STILL moving forward.

"Black Men Holding Hands"

Grab your brother's hand
It's common in Africa
Better together.

freedom clay

"Racism Isn't Blind"

Racial division
Still exist in our country
So pay attention.

"Children of the World"

Tomorrow's promise
Looking into the future
Take good care of us.

"Medicinal Balm"

Healing properties
With outstretched hands cover us
With love, grace and strength.

United, We Heal"

Let's mourn together
Against ALL injustices
Black folks have endured.

freedom clay

"Moving Forward"

Standing in the light
Thinking of my ancestors
And how they pressed on...

"Umoja"

Solidarity
It's interconnectedness
Active harmony.

"Spiritual Cleansing"

I'm cleansing the air
With my smudge stick and feather
Removing toxins.

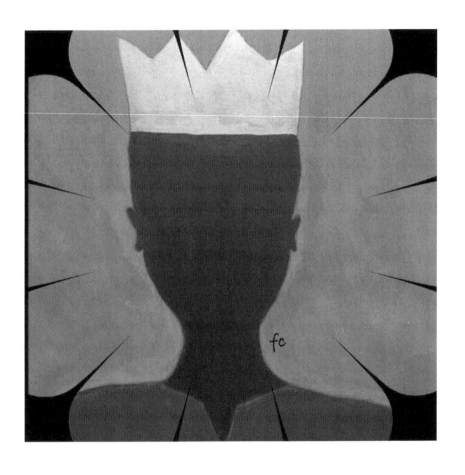

freedom clay

"King Holiday"

Majestic reigning
In aligned or tilted crowns
We are "Dope Black Kings".

"Shades of Royalty"

Thinking royal thoughts
of ancestral kings and queens
Humanity reigns.

"Queen Sugar"

The taste of a queen
Bittersweet deliciousness
It's insatiable.

"Natural Beauties"

"Organic Beauties"
In a world full of filters
They are filter free.

"The Visible Crown"

Wrapped in "valued" gold
Against ALL odds, we're winning
Black men rock red crowns.

"Moving While Heavy-Laden"

When you're burdened down
KNOW your crown is paid in full
Sit and rest, young prince.

freedom clay

"Sun-kissed Boys"

Kissed by the sun's rays.
Black boy joy can't be contained
Boundlessly leaping.

"Black Boy Joy"

His infectious laugh
Sounds like a sweet melody
That's life affirming.

freedom clay

"Professor Bluez"

He is Black and bright
With focus and direction
That was then and now.

"Sound the Alarm"

A Black man's magic
Emits orange smoke signals
Like rays of sunshine.

"Black Boy Panther Magic"

He's a PROUD Black boy
And a fan of Black Panther
Who dreams in color.

"Let Black Boys Be Boys"

Children do embrace
Black boys are affectionate
Human connection.

freedom clay

"Marble Play in Sunday Jackets"

Black boys love to play
Regardless of resources
Just creative minds.

"Brothaz in Hats"

Black men and their hats
Is a whole serious thing
During ALL seasons.

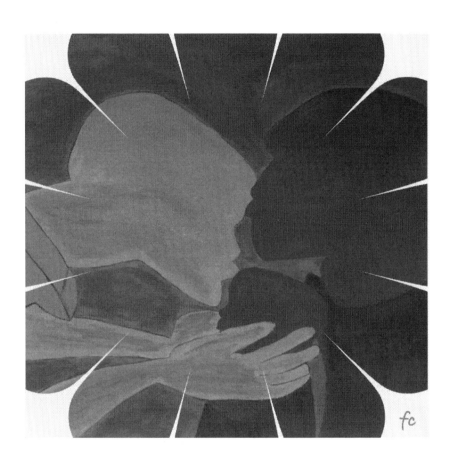

"3 Generations of Love, Hope & Life"

Black men love their sons
By modeling affection
That's life sustaining.

"Black Men Love"

Three generations
Of demonstrated Black love
Between Dads and sons.

"A Father's Day Salute"

Good Fathers exist
Today, we celebrate YOU
For ALL that YOU do.

"Like Father, Like Son"

He looks up to YOU
You're his first superhero
And his protector.

"Legacy I"

Life contributions
Benefiting humankind
With grace and purpose.

"Legacy II"

Your contributions
Designed to make lives better
With highest regards.

"Love, Loyalty & Legacy"

Love with ALL your heart
Lead with purposed loyalty
This is legacy.

"Veterans Salute"

For ALL who have served
You are appreciated
Freedom isn't free.

"Re-membering Pac"

Prophetic black rose
Tupac Amaru Shakur
He thrived in concrete.

"A Love Supreme"

Roots in High Peezy
Known for composing "free" jazz
He is John Coltrane.

"Remembering Bill Withers"

You can "lean on me".
Let's create a "lovely day"
Rest well, Bill Withers.

"Three of My Heroes: Say Their Names"

Nelson Mandela
His name is Bayard Rustin
and "the" James Baldwin.

"Son of Sir Bayard"

Still not widely known
Prophet of humanity
Freedom & justice.

"Dapper Dan's Jewels"

Follow the culture
With "exceptionalism"
and global insight.

"The Manifestation of King's Dream"

He wasn't afraid
To ask for what he needed
So he received it.

"1/28/20"

Global gloominess
Can be transformed with healing
And acknowledgement.

"Kobe Bryant"

A young trailblazer
Who excelled on/off the court
He's legendary.

"Remembering Langston"

He knew down and out
He understood the struggle
Yet, he kept rising.

"A Political Tour De Force"

Elijah Cummings
A humanitarian
Made a difference.

"Re-membering Malcom X"

Applied resistance
Was a way of life for him
Known as Malcom X.

"Haiku for the Prince"

Many "adore" "kiss'",
Sometimes it snows in April
Watching "Purple Rain".

freedom clay

"Ron Simmons"

Black Visionary
And a gay luminary
Left a legacy.

"Dr. Otis Tillman, Sr."

A man of standard
A healer and activist
Made a difference.

"Congressman John Lewis"

Civil Rights icon
And longtime freedom fighter
Farewell, great servant.

"Remembering John Singleton"

From "Boyz n the Hood"
To days of "Higher Learning"
"Poetic Justice".

"Nipsey Hussle"

The skinny MOGUL
Has left a profound impact
On many strangers.

"Buddy Bolden"

The Father of Jazz
He was heavy in the head
Remember his name.

"Nigel Shelby"

It is a damn shame
Bullying ended his life
Because he was FREE.

"Happy 70th Personal New Year, Stevie"

One of the greatest
Musical luminaries
And blindingly bright.

freedom clay

"L-O-V-E"

It's like breathing air
We cannot thrive without it
Love is essential.

"Puppy Love"

She ran up to me
Out of nowhere with pure love
And my heart melted.

"I Call Them Love"

What do you call them
An open-ended question
This was the answer.

"You Are Loved"

Somebody loves YOU
In spite of everything
Find peace in this truth.

freedom clay

"Love is Love II"

Love can't be contained
It presents in many forms
BE love; receive love.

"Love Unlimited"

BE open to hope
As long as you are breathing
Hope is a lifeline.

freedom clay

"Love Matters"

BE open to love
As long as you are breathing
Love is a lifeline.

"Open Hearted Love"

BE open to love
Don't focus on how and when
Just open the door.

"Love is Love"

Everybody
Under the sun, moon and stars
Deserves to be loved.

"Loving Reminder"

Somebody loves YOU
You have always been the one
Just because you're YOU.

"Bonding Moments"

Sit down and relax
And engage in healing touch
LOVE responsibly.

"Love and Humanity"

Love will beckon love
Faithfully with open arms
Void of perfection.

freedom clay

"Infinite Possibilities"

Tell me who you are
I will show you who I am
We'll see what happens.

"Face 2 Face"

Be willing to see
What resides in you & me
Powerful, we are.

"Seeing eye 2 eye"

We saw each other
Because flowers have eyes too
Take the time to see.

"Compassion"

Thinking beyond self
Responding to someone's plight
Without judging them.

"Love Begets Love"

Let's make love right now
It is the beauty of hope
Sow it, then reap it.

"Sexual Discourse"

Sex is like a drug
It can be medicinal
And lethal 4 some.

"Love Calls"

Where are you right now
I'm trying to get to you
I will be waiting.

"Love Answers"

Answering your call
You have my number; use it
I never left home.

"The Photograph"

Love can be heavy
Like weighted bricks on your chest
Yield into the feelings.

"The Cock Takes No Bull"

The rooster and bull
Don't always see eye 2 eye
Yet, they co-exist.

"Word-Up"

They are "tone" setters
Powerful beyond measure
Choose and speak with care.

"Love & Respect"

They go hand in hand
Like rainbows and promises
Like peaches and cream.

"Respect"

Sometimes, it is earned
Other times it's simply shown
It's humane action.

"Re-connecting"

Circular moments
It's reunification
Aligned vibrations.

"A Vision of Love, Healing and Unity"

We can live freely
When love, pain, healing unite
Under life's one roof.

"Elevated Brightness"

Lifting up our lights
In dark spaces together
Provides clarity.

"Love Heals"

Healing should take place
In healthy relationships
Along with magic.

"Heart Care"

Take care of your heart
Because we only have one
Treating it with love.

"Cozy Love"

Loving expressions
Should be exercised daily
Now, go hug someone.

"Intercessory Prayer"

Before you retire
Say a prayer for someone
Other than yourself.

freedom clay

"Reaching Out"

High five to hand-up
It's not about a hand-out
A hand-up matters.

"Be the Example"

Yes, do as I say
More importantly, model
What I am doing.

"I see YOU"

Feeling like a dot
In our gargantuan world
Yet, I'm always watched.

"Concealed Flowers"

Men love flowers too
Toxic masculinity
Has silenced this truth.

"Bald, Black, Queer & Here"

The intersections
Of bald, Black, queer and brilliant
Are overwhelming.

"Trans-Huemans Matter"

Let me be real clear
About inclusivity
Black trans lives matter!

"Pride Month"

Love is rainbow rays
With celebrations of PRIDE
Highlighted in June.

"Red"

The color of love
A holiday favorite
Visual power.

"Black Is the Color of Pride"

Be real black for me
Is a testament to strength
And collective pride.

"Pondering Blackness"

The meaning of Black
Black is more than a color
It's political.

"Green Is..."

My pasture is green
Because I stay hydrated
It's reproduction.

"Shades of Life"

Up above my head
The trees are green and shady
And it gives me LIFE.

"Path of Hope"

When nature reveals
Green is the color of LIFE
It's a sign of hope.

"Joy & Peace"

It's the simple things
That enhance my joy and peace
Like art & coffee.

freedom clay

"Black Art"

Black art in motion
Having artsy dialogue
Pérez Art Museum.

"African Mask"

Keeper of secrets
Absorbs gloomy energy
And beautiful art.

"Coffee and the Sounds of Music"

Afternoon coffee
And the sounds of birds chirping
Sitting on my deck.

"When Coffee Conjures Hope"

Coffee reflections
Fostering meditations
Of hope, love and peace.

"Jazzy Perspectives"

International
A fusion of melodies
With some dissonance.

"Jazz"

Complicated sounds
Intertwining melodies
Doing the tango.

"Black History"

Black History is
American history
Just like JAZZ music.

"Sounds of the Times"

The saxophone man
Playing jazzy dissonance
Reflecting the times.

"Rocketman"

He is still standing
True love is hard to come by
His name is Elton.

"Seattle's Finest"

He's swaggalicious
Serving pimp daddy realnezz
With dyeable shoes.

freedom clay

"Black Men Can Jump"

Black man in pigtails
can levitate and catch balls
The magic is real.

"Hoop Dreamz"

Looking up in awe
With great anticipation
To secure the WIN.

"The Afro Graduates"

A goal completed
Destined to open more doors
For "us" to walk through...

"Man Down"

The morning after
The conversations ensued
Embrace new moments.

"Guardian Angel"

They were in harm's way
A Benevolent Stranger
Valued their being.

"Ms Soul 2 Soul"

Wherever I go
"Ms. Soul 2 Soul" has my back
There's comfort in that.

"Earth Angels"

Serving as lifeguards
Their wings are invisible
While elevating.

"Mine Eyes"

Described as piercing
Exploring beyond the veil
I'm a "SOUL" watcher.

"Curiosity"

A sense of wonder
Unbridled exploration
Curiosity.

"7/5/19"

Take the time to be
Acknowledge yourself daily
It's necessary.

"7/14/19"

Today I was told
My collection of haiku
Is a healing tool.

"7/19/19"

2019
Balance and recovery
Made a difference.

"7/27/19"

A hurtful feeling
When one is violated
Trust is compromised.

"8/7/19"

Make time for laughter
That sounds like speakable joy
And feels like sunshine.

"Recovery"

Blooming thru concrete
Like a rose thirsting for light
Healed by rays of SUN.

"Vino Rojo"

I am savoring
The notes and flavor profile
Of a good red wine.

"Haiku Day: 4/17/20"

It's a special day
And seventeen syllables
Are the reasons why.

"Haiku Dreams"

When I am sleeping
Sometimes, I dream in haiku
Succinct poetry.

"Dreaming"

I dream in haiku
Of a world without borders
I'm a believer.

"Autism Speaks"

Socially unique
Speaking the unfiltered truth
with consistency.

freedom clay

"Boundless Blessings"

Pray for their increase
It won't devalue your worth.
There's enough for ALL.

"Saturday Slumber"

Listening to the rain
Create skylight rhythms
Soothing to my soul.

"Relax & Snuggle"

Rainy day snuggles
Are restorative blessings
Relax and enjoy.

"Super Soul Sundays"

Reflective moments
Focusing on the present
With a grateful heart.

"Soulful Sundays"

Days of reverence
Intentional Reflections
Super soul Sundays.

"WAIT"

Why am I talking
Practice the art of waiting
Breathe and BE patient.

freedom clay

"Time Limited"

Say what you feel now
The next day may be too late
God's timing is REAL.

"Reality Is…"

My reality
Isn't consumed by your past
It's focused on NOW.

"Blind Faith"

Dance in the darkness
Like blindness doesn't exist
Until you see light.

"Twilight Moments"

Sunny is the light
And dark is the evening
Where do you fit in?

"Shadow Work"

Reflections are REAL
Do you see yourself in them?
Pay close attention.

"Ego Adjustment"

He took his crown off
To adjust his big ego
Then put it back on.

freedom clay

"EGO Check"

Do not ease God out
Just to appease your ego
Let love be your guide.

"Bandage Art"

Had a lil boo boo
So I earned my bandages
My badge of honor.

"Peace Be Still"

My mind is racing
Without a destination
To secure refuge.

"Closeted Thoughts"

All thoughts in our head
Are not meant to be spoken
Don't be "insecure".

freedom clay

"Anticipating Dance"

Sitting here thinking
I can't wait to dance with you
It will come to pass.

"Green Book"

Book of resources
Designed for Black travelers
Pre-integration.

freedom clay

"Sunny Possibilities"

The sun is shining
With bright possibilities
Take time to enjoy.

"God's Grace"

Absorbing the light
Standing in awe of God's Grace
It is sufficient.

"Earth Angels"

Divine light forces
They are encamped around us
God's earthly soldiers.

"Unconditional Gratitude & Praise"

Thanksgiving matters
Regardless of the season
I will lift my hands.

"Bright Disposition"

My joy is boundless
And my sunny countenance
Keeps the clouds at bay.

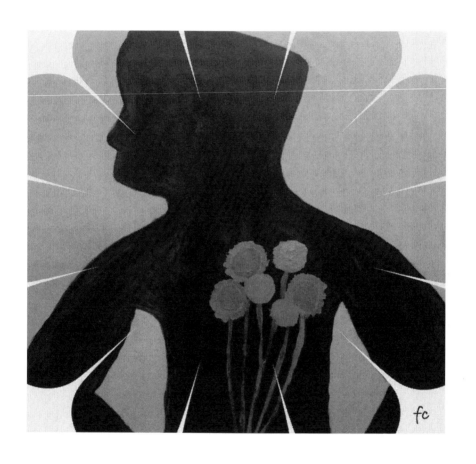

freedom clay

"Handpicked Flowers"

I have a surprise
They're hiding behind my back
I hope you likey.

"Single Autumn Rose"

Give "the one" a rose
Who makes your heart sings today
Later may not come.

freedom clay

"My Perennial Golden Rayed Lily"

You return yearly
With specific messages
On faith, hope and grace.

"Sunflower JOY"

I flirted with joy
In a field of sunflowers
And it felt so good.

freedom clay

"Flowers & Bees"

Both are life sources
With sweet sensibilities
Yet, one can sting YOU.

"Flowers In-Motion"

Blowing in the wind
Their beauty was arrested
To re-visit LIFE.

"Clouds"

Angelic art forms
Created by The Most High
Observed in the sky.

"Multi-level Clouds"

Up above the clouds
There are more clouds that exist
So let's aim higher.

"Azul Sky"

The sun is setting
And the moon is apparent
Among azul sky.

"Cigar Bluez"

Glorious blue sky
On this lit Thursday evening
Exhaling only.

"The Nest"

It served its purpose
Eggs laid, nurtured and hatched
The circle of life.

"The Tree of Life"

Arms outstretched widely
Standing PROUD under the tree
The color of life.

"Suspended Red Leaf"

Seemingly alone
Yet still attached to the vine
Perception matters.

"Waves"

All we have is NOW
And the waves of life will come
Faithfully ride them.

freedom clay

"Rainfall"

The rain is falling
Feeling the cleansing effects
A restoration.

"Transitional Beauties"

Once caterpillars
Now colorful butterflies
Metamorphosis.

"Mystic Waters"

Still waters run deep
When mystique is magical
And love is endless.

"Water, Hugs & Vulnerability"

Descending water
Is restoring like a hug
In an unsafe world.

"Bright Stars"

My constellation
Is filled with many bright stars
Magical, they are.

"Regeneration"

As spring approaches
Pruning is necessary
To reveal new growth.

"Stepping into Fall"

I love autumn walks
Taking in the warm colors
Indicating change.

"Moving with a Purpose"

Walking for my health
And taking in the beauty
Of bright spring flowers.

"Conversations with Nature"

Commune with nature
Converse with flowers and trees
They see and hear too.

"Power in the Blood"

The blood, sweat and tears
Experienced in the fields
Yielded fruitful crops.

"Relatively"

Time, distance and space
All have meaning and value
It's ALL relative.

"Popsicle Bluez"

Well, whaddup July
Hot fun in the summatime
Popsicle in hand.

"Cuba"

Beautiful ruins
Many colors of Black pride
The poor are so RICH.

"Jazzy Disposition"

I see jazz in you
Non-lyrical melodies
That's soothing my soul.

freedom clay

"Cherish the Moment"

Blow in like the wind
Fleeting like day turns to nite
Stay for a minute.

"Jewel Being"

A jewel, YOU are
Let me find refuge in you
You are endearing.

"Long Live the Dream"

Ninety years ago
A majestic "King" was born
And the dream lives on.

"Bridge Building"

I'm building bridges
Enduring the test of time
With "sankofa" tools.

freedom clay

"Masked Reality"

Unmasking the truth
You cannot hide from yourself
Now, show up for YOU.

"Lady Barbara Alston"

With grace, peace and style
She lovingly served others
Compassionately.

"Beale Street Talk"

Passionately told
An intimate love story
Of shackled freedom.

"Tagged"

I've been targeted
What does it mean to be tagged
Now, I'm wondering.

"Good Morning"

It's a brand new start
The beginning of greatness
It starts in the mind.

"Soundz of Blacknezz"

It's a symphony
Harmonious dissonance
Put it on repeat.

"Orchestrated Prayers"

God, my Conductor
Let me be your symphony
Direct me, Oh Lord.

"2019: The Year of Freedom"

Moving with focus
Better days are ahead now
The year of freedom.

"Umoja"

Cooperative
Intentional relations
Building together.

"Christmas Memories"

Christmas time is here
I'm grateful for memories
Together, we had.

"Jingle Amor"

Love is the reason
For the holiday season
So jingle the bells.

"Holiday Snow"

Serenely falling
Blanketing the neighborhood
The Most High's Painting.

freedom clay

"Questions"

What, when, where and how
We often query ourselves
Still with no answers.

"Morning Glory"

Lifter of my head
I see the colors of life
I am standing tall.

freedom clay

"Mama's Museum"

Filled with memories
Of past, present and future
Your presence is felt.

"927 Mayford Drive"

I wasn't raised here
Then a connection ensued
A "peace" of Mama.

freedom clay

"Summer 2019"

The place I've called home
Purging and being restored
Town of Kernersville.

"Angelic Voice"

I'm hearing your voice
Telling me to be STILL now
I go and sit down.

"Reflections I"

Seeing me in We
Is the consummate blessing
Familial ties bind.

"Reflections II"

Looking back at me
Unafraid of my shadow
I'm a dream fulfilled.

"Reflections of Life"

Life is so fleeting
Minutes cannot be contained
Live in the present.

"Reflections of Time"

Why are we waiting
Time doesn't belong to us
Nor does the future.

freedom clay

"Reflections of Life & Time"

We can't make it last
So choose to live in real time
Now is all we got.

"Healing"

Addressing the pain
It takes time to recover
Don't rush the process.

"Grief is Love"

My salute with love
To all those who are grieving
Take your time and heal.

"Heart Beating"

My heart is mending
While beating through grief and loss
Resilient, it is.

freedom clay

"My Celestial Angels"

I am my Mom's son
And my grandmother's grandson
I represent them.

"Grief I"

Amplified sadness
Ignited by profound loss
Make meaning of it.

"Grief II"

It's like a slow burn
That requires time for healing
You cannot rush it.

"A Prayer for Healing"

Bless those who aren't well
They may be fighting to heal
Undiscovered wounds.

"Blessed Trinity"

I saw love today
In the face of sunflowers
Salute to Mama.

"Cardinal Love"

I saw my mama
Sitting on the windowsill
Looking right at me.

freedom clay

"Bright & Colorful Life"

I saw you today
And you summoned me to you
And I responded.

"True Story"

Just woke up from nap
My Mother visited me
And hugged me tightly.

freedom clay

"My Heart Beat"

My heart is beating
With her blood flowing thru me
I'm her legacy.

"Mother & Son Chronicles"

Son asked Mom to dance
Mom was resistant, at first
Then she relented.

freedom clay

"Mama's aka NeNe's Bug"

It's a piece of you
I decided to keep it
Because I LOVE YOU.

"Tipping Our Hats Off To YOU Nana"

We honored your life
Hats were worn to extol you
We love YOU, Nana.

freedom clay

"3rd of December"

I'm thinking of YOU
Today, it has been five months
My infinite Love.

"7 months"

It's been seven months
A number of completion
Feels like yesterday.

freedom clay

"8 months"

Sometimes, I hear you
In my dreams very clearly
Only to wake up.

"5/3/19"

Still making meaning
Of my loss ten months ago
It takes time to heal.

"6/3/19"

Time waits 4 no one
It has been 11 months
Loving YOU dearly.

"8/11/19"

Indelible marks
She left like tribal tattoos
Unforgettable.

"730 days aka 2 years"

Her name is Constance
She's 4ver my Mother
Today makes 2 years.

"Leo Locs"

My mane; my glory
Thick, strong, bold and colorful
Zion the Lion.

"Zion the Leo Lion"

My mane is textured
With strong emerald green eyes
Colorful and free.

"7/23-8/22"

Royalty Season
It's a whole majestic mood
It's our time to SHINE.

"Leo Season 2020"

Our season is here
To shine like never before
Because we made it!!!

"Message to Baby freedom clay"

You have God's favor
Reigning over your WHOLE life
So proceed in peace.

"Chapter 47"

Live, love and let live
It is my time and season
Onward and upward.

"My Laughter"

It is infectious
I laugh fully and deeply
It is from my heart.

freedom clay

"freedom's prerogative"

I know the standard
Of American haiku
Yet, I choose my way.

"Crown of Roses"

Adorned with roses
He's covered and protected
Majestically.

freedom clay

"Haiku Luva"

Still my haiku boo
Making love thru structured words
It's pure ecstasy.

"Acknowledgement"

You were a vessel
And nothing more; nothing less
Kindly, I thank you.

freedom clay

"Thank You"

It's only two words
To express one's gratitude
Yet, they mean so much.

"Re-Imagining Freedom"

Re-Imagining
What freedom looks like today
With hopeful visions.

epilogue

Black men and boys of ALL shades regardless of our upbringing, educational status, socioeconomic status, sexual orientation, etc. have been or will experience being racially profiled and discriminated against knowingly and/or unknowingly in our lifetime. This constant pressure and indictment on our "hue-manity" can be exhausting; therefore, taking a toll on our physical, mental/emotional and spiritual wellbeing. Furthermore, impacting our relationship with ourselves and our relationships with others. This is why it is vital to our existence that we love ourselves and each other completely and unapologetically in a world that has shown us time and time again that we aren't loved or valued. All human-beings will experience the "blues" in some capacity; however, their blues can NEVER be compared to ours.

This "peace" is lovingly dedicated to ALL Black men and boys who have experienced the blues carrying the weight of the world unfairly chiefly because of the "hue" of our skin. I see YOU/US and you/we are loved and valued against ALL odds, so wear your "floral" crown PROUDLY. It's a beautiful symbol of life and our respective lives lived will become our legacies. There is immortal "LIFE" in our respective legacies.

about the author

freedom clay is an internationally recognized visual creative and poet. He's a passionate lover of life. This is freedom clay's third published book. His first book, "Inspirational and Provocative Moments on Faith, Self-Love & Relationships" listed as a bestseller during the first week of release and his second book, "575: a collection of haiku by freedom clay" has been heralded as a remarkable literary work.

He resides in Durham, NC.

Social Media Platforms:
IG: freedom-clay
Twitter:@freedomclay
Facebook: Afro Folk Art and Photography by freedom clay

"Colors of Victory Intersecting Dis-ease-19" aka "COVID-19"

"And So It Is..."
Lawd, we will get by
I'm thanking you in advance
For what is to come.

Made in the USA
Columbia, SC
18 April 2023

15542683R00213